C000132960

THE LITTLE
SHERRY
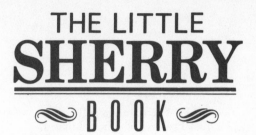
∞ BOOK ∞

Jennie Reekie

PIATKUS

© 1988 Judy Piatkus (Publishers) Limited

First published in 1988 by
Judy Piatkus (Publishers) Limited,
5 Windmill Street, London W1P 1HF

British Library Cataloguing in Publication Data
Reekie, Jennie
The little sherry book.
1. Sherry
I. Title
641.2'2

ISBN 0-86188-763-8

Drawings by Trevor Newton
Designed by Susan Ryall
Cover photograph by Theo Bergström

Phototypeset in 10 on 11pt Linotron Plantin by
Phoenix Photosetting, Chatham
Printed and bound in Great Britain by
The Bath Press, Avon

CONTENTS

Viña Bristol,
a Harvey vineyard
near Jerez.

A SHORT HISTORY OF SHERRY

Over 3,000 years ago the Phoenicians conquered the Iberian peninsula and founded, among other colonies, Gadir (now Cadiz) and Xera (Jerez), where they planted vines. Their invasion was followed by that of the Greeks whose viticulture and love of wine is well documented, and by the time the Romans arrived the wine trade in this area was flourishing. Certet, as they renamed Xera, became an important centre and wine from the region was exported throughout the Roman Empire, causing some upset amongst the Italian wine growers who demanded a limit on the number of new vines being planted in this far corner of the known globe.

After the collapse of the Roman Empire, which had provided comparative stability, Spain's history became as turbulent as that of its other European counterparts which had previously formed part of the Empire. Roman dominance was replaced by the encroachments of various branches of a Teutonic tribe called the Vandals, whose only lasting claim to fame is that they christened the south-west corner of Spain Vandalusia, as it is still called but without the 'V'. They were supplanted by the Visigoths, then the Berbers and eventually the Moors, whose influence remains clearly visible today.

With countless campaigns being waged across them, as was to happen again in later wars, the vine-yards suffered considerable damage, but under the Moors they were gradually replanted. This may seem surprising in view of the Muslim faith's ban on alcohol, but the conquerors ate the natural products of fresh grapes and raisins and appear to have been happy enough to let their Christian subjects enjoy their own infidel habits!

The Moors were finally defeated by Spanish Catholic Princes towards the end of the thirteenth century. The story is told that the first king, Alphonse X The Wise, set about re-establishing the area as a wine centre by giving land to 300 of his noblemen and personally pruning many of the vines as an example to them.

It is possible that trade in wine between England and Spain began while the Moors were still in occupation, but there is definite evidence that it was flourishing by the middle of the fourteenth century. Chaucer refers to the 'white wine of Lepe' in the Pardoner's Tale, and it is clear from his advice to

steer clear of it since it was so much stronger than other wines that it was already being fortified. The purpose of fortifying wine by adding neat alcohol (generally brandy in the case of sherry) was to improve the keeping qualities of the wine and help it to travel better. Wine-making was much more of a hit and miss affair then, with casks frequently oxidising and turning to vinegar, and the success of sherry in England must in part have been due to the fact that it arrived in much better condition than unfortified wines that were sent from France or northern Spain.

The hot Mediterranean climate also played a part in this success, as the sun increases the amount of

Sun drying grapes on esparto mats

sugar in the grapes and, consequently, the alcohol content of the wine, resulting in wines with better keeping qualities.

In view of the important role British merchants were to play in the development of the sherry industry over the next 600 years, it is of historical interest that the trade between the two countries would never have started, let alone blossomed, if this area of Spain had not been able to supply one of Britain's most pressing needs of the time – salt, from the Mediterranean. It would appear that this, initially, was the most important export, with the wine merely being used as ballast.

In 1492 the Catholic Princes ordered the expulsion of the Jews from Spain. The traditional merchants in every country they lived in, their place was quickly filled by a number of foreign, and especially

4

British, merchants. By the middle of the sixteenth century, many of the British contingent were Catholics fleeing the Protestant England of Henry VIII, while in later centuries it was to be French aristocrats escaping the Revolution as well as French Huguenot refugees.

By the time Elizabeth I came to the throne, sherris-sack, or sack as it was more frequently referred to, was a common drink. Sherris was, of course, a corruption of Jerez where the wine originated, whilst sack came from the Spanish *sacar* meaning wines for export. Shakespeare, through the person of Sir John Falstaff, eulogised sherry more fulsomely than has any other poet before or since:

'A good sherris-sack hath a two-fold operation in it. It ascends me into the brain; dries me there all the

foolish and dull and crudy vapours which environ it
. . . The second property of your excellent sherris
is, the warming of the blood; which before cold and
settled, left the liver white and pale, which is the
badge of pusillanimity and cowardice; but the sherris warms it and makes it course from the inwards to
the parts extreme . . . Hereof comes it that Prince
Harry is valiant; for the cold blood he did naturally
inherit of his father, he hath, like lean, sterile and
bare land, manured, husbanded and tilled, with
excellent endeavour of drinking good and good store
of fertile sherris, that he is become hot and valiant; if
I had a thousand sons, the first human principle I
would teach them should be, to forswear thin
potations and to addict themselves to sack.'

* * *

These were troubled times, though, for the trade in general. Whilst some British merchants continued to live in Jerez, Drake's blockade of the Spanish ports was hardly conducive to good trading relations – though his raid on Cadiz possibly did more to increase sherry-drinking in England than any other single act. He seized 2,900 pipes (these were just a little larger than the average butt which contains in the region of 110 gallons) of sherry that were lying on the harbour quay and whisked them back to England, where his booty was received with great glee.

Samuel Pepys enjoyed drinking sherry and visited Jerez in 1683. Previously, in 1662, together with three friends, he had bought two butts of sherry and recorded in his diary that his portion was 'put into a hogshead, and the vessel filled up with four gallons of Malaga Wine, but what it will stand us in I know not; but it is the first great quantity of wine that I ever bought'. On another occasion, before an important court case, he wrote in his diary: 'To comfort myself did go to the Dog and drink half a pint of mulled sack.'

*   *   *

With peace came a long period of prosperity, during which time many of the old established sherry houses were set up, only to be disrupted again by the Peninsular War when many of the vineyards were completely destroyed. It was this sorry state of affairs which caused the schoolboy John Ruskin

(1819-1900), whose father was in partnership with Pedro Domecq, to write:

> Alas, and it filled me with grief
> To see there no promise of fruit
> For the insect was eating the leaf
> And the worm was at work on the root.
> Neglected for many a year,
> Unpruned and untended they hung,
> The leafage was withered and sere,
> And the vineyards looked sad in the sun.
>
> No wine had attained to old age here,
> It was new, it was sour, it was dead.
> Oh, here was no voice of the gauger;
> Nor sound of the cellarman's tread.

Following the defeat of Napoleon's armies, the sherry industry went through one of its greatest periods of expansion. The art of sherry-making was perfected, the solera system (see page 21) was introduced, resulting in a far greater degree of consistency in the wines, and vast warehouses or bodegas were built.

By the 1870s no English sideboard was complete without its decanter of sherry, and sherry was drunk throughout the length and breadth of Britain as well as in the furthest outposts of her Empire. Regrettably, the demands of this very success resulted in some extremely mediocre, and indeed downright

bad, wines being shipped which did little in the long term to enhance sherry's reputation. Nor did the practice of some wine merchants and grocers of mixing their own 'sherries', many of which bore little or no relation to the genuine article.

Success was followed by catastrophic failure of the worst kind. In 1863, in a greenhouse in Hammersmith, an American aphid – phylloxera – was discovered and proceeded to work its way across Europe decimating all the old vineyards. Malaga was hit in 1875. For a while it looked as if the vineyards of Jerez might have escaped the plague, but twenty years later they too succumbed and were totally wiped out.

Being a slow-maturing wine there were, luckily, enough stocks of sherry to ensure, if not a plentiful supply, at least a slow and steady output over the twenty years or so it took to restock the vineyards. By the 1930s, when it became a popular and fashionable drink again in England, stocks were sufficiently well recovered to ensure that there was never a

shortage. Fortunately, neither the Spanish Civil War nor the Second World War created too much havoc in the vineyards, although there was, naturally, little wine exported during that time.

Between 1965 and 1972 there was a boom in sherry-drinking, but the following years showed a considerable decline, not only in England but throughout the world. This has gradually been reversed, but whereas at one time the sweeter sherries were more popular, it is now the finos and the even drier manzanillas which are increasing their share of the market.

SHERRY IN THE USA

When Christopher Columbus set out on his voyage across the Atlantic to discover the New World, he sailed from the Guadalquivir River. Most of his seamen were local Andalusians – many indeed were Jerezanos – and his well-provisioned ships had plentiful supplies of sherry on board. Sherry is, therefore, thought to be if not the first then certainly one of the first wines ever to enter the United States of America.

On his third journey in 1498, when he set out to discover the island of Trinidad, Columbus sailed from Sanlúcar de Barrameda and in the sixteenth century this became one of the most important trading ports for the New World.

WHY SHERRY
IS UNIQUE

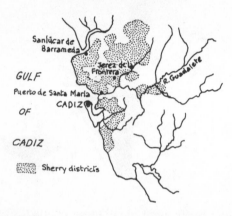

The only area in the world where sherry can be produced is within a triangle formed by the towns of Jerez de la Frontera, El Puerto de Santa Maria and Sanlúcar de Barrameda. To the north of the triangle is the Guadalquivir River and the south is bordered by the mouth of the Guadalete. Even if identical vines are grown in another area with a similar climate, and the wine-making process is carried out in exactly the same way, the end result will have different characteristics to a true sherry.

There are a number of reasons for this, including the optimum climate for the grapes – 70 days of rainfall and 295 of sunshine (which they generally achieve), and the light sea breezes from the Atlantic – but there are two main ones. The first is the soil in which the vines are grown. Not all, but the majority, of the vineyards are planted on soil known as 'albariza' which has a very high calcium carbonate or chalk content. This soil is able to absorb the torrential winter rains and then, unlike other soils which cake and crack in the heat, forms a crust which protects the roots of the vines and slowly releases the water to them. This gives the grapes plenty of nourishment, despite the intense sunshine which ripens them so well.

The second reason is the development of a yeast-like mould or 'flor', as it is known, on the top of the wine while it is maturing in the cask. The greater the development of flor, the lighter and drier the sherry, with the heavier olorosos producing virtually no flor at all. A totally natural occurrence in this small region of Spain and in the Jura mountains of France, flor cannot be induced to grow on wines in any other part of the world and it is this flor which imparts the slight yeasty flavour which characterises a good fino sherry.

OTHER FORTIFIED WINES

A number of countries including Britain, South Africa, Australia, the USA and Cyprus all produce wines which closely resemble genuine sherries from Spain, but for the reasons given above cannot be classified as true sherries.

So-called British sherry is not a natural wine but a 'made' wine manufactured in England from imported concentrated grape must that is reconstituted, fortified and sweetened.

There, in Jerez, drink the famous wine at its source.

Lord Byron

Long live sherry! Jerez is a town which should be in Paradise.

Victor Hugo

CULTIVATION OF THE GRAPES

The two kinds of grape most commonly used for sherry are the Palomino de Jerez and Pedro Ximenez, the latter being used for the sweeter wines. In a few of the older vineyards there are still a few Moscatel vines remaining, and these also give a sweeter wine.

Following the devastation caused by phylloxera at the end of the last century, all the vines are now produced by grafting the Palomino or Pedro Ximenez on to American root stock which is resistant to the phylloxera aphid. The vines can bear fruit within a year or two, but the flowers are cut off so that the grapes cannot develop, to enable the vine to become sturdier and stronger. It is not until the vine is in its fourth or fifth year that a crop is harvested from it, and some sherry houses prefer the vines to be a minimum of eight years old.

During the next twenty to twenty-five years the vine gives its highest yield and best quality grapes. While capable of producing grapes for fifty years or more, both the quality and the yield decrease after twenty-five to thirty years and the majority of vines are replaced at this age.

Vines require careful attention throughout the year if they are to produce good grapes. In October, after the harvest, some of the earth is dug out from the roots and used to make a wall round the vine so that all the rainwater is captured and does not simply run off the soil. In spring, after the rains, this is replaced but it must always be kept loose and well-harrowed. Weeds also present a problem and must be kept under control or they will sap the moisture and goodness from the soil. At one time all this work had to be carried out manually, but these days most of the vineyards are highly mechanised and much of the work is carried out by machines. However, highly skilled tasks, such as pruning, are still done by hand.

HARVESTING AND PRESSING THE GRAPES

The first week in September usually sees the start of the grape harvest, which lasts for about three weeks. In some years it has been known to begin in late August, while occasionally it is mid-September before the grapes are ripe enough to harvest. Picking is still carried out by hand, but while at one time the grapes were pressed at the vineyard, they are now generally loaded on to lorries and sent to one of the three sherry towns for pressing there.

Improved techniques for gauging the exact ripeness of the fruit means that it is no longer essential to leave the Palomino grapes out in the sun for several hours, although some vineyards still like to do this. 'Sunning' concentrates the grape juice and increases the sugar content and is vital for the production of sweet wines from the Pedro Ximenez and Moscatel grapes. The grapes are laid out on grass mats for several days and are just lightly covered at night to protect them from dew.

Treading the grapes with nail-studded boots in a large trough is now a thing of the past except at ceremonial occasions, and it is now all done by machine. For many years the 'must' or grape juice produced by machines was considered to be inferior to that produced by treading, but with advances in technology the reverse is now true.

Prior to pressing, the grapes are first sprinkled with gypsum, a practice know as plastering which improves the quality of the must and assists fermentation. In Victorian England considerable concern was expressed over this in medical circles as it was felt it could be detrimental to health. Countless treatises were written on the subject, but by the end of the nineteenth century it had finally been proved that these fears were groundless.

If penicillin cures illnesses, sherry resuscitates the dead.

Dr. Alexander Fleming

How Sherry Is Produced

Immediately the grapes have been pressed the must is poured into new oak casks so that they are just over three-quarters full, and it starts fermenting naturally almost at once. For the next three or four days there is very vigorous fermentation as the must froths and bubbles. This gradually dies down, and it continues to ferment slowly for the next ten weeks during which time all the sugar in the grapes turns to alcohol.

By January the wine has generally cleared, with all the sediment sinking to the bottom of the butt to form the 'lees'. The development of flor (see page 13) often starts at eight to ten weeks, but sometimes it is not until the following spring that this yeasty mould appears. To encourage the flor to develop, the butts are not tightly bunged but are left open, and unlike other wines which are stored and matured in underground cellars, the sherry is stored above ground in light, airy bodegas (warehouses).

The unusual property of sherry is that two apparently identical butts of wine from the same vineyard, situated in the same part of a bodega, can develop in entirely different ways with one eventually turning into a light fino and the other into a rich, full-bodied oloroso. If allowed to develop in this way as unblended wines or *anadas*, good wines can be and are produced but it is virtually impossible to have any kind of consistency. This is important both for the shipper and for the consumer, as repeat orders could not be made. Even if the wine were blended it would be impossible to match it exactly.

THE SOLERA SYSTEM

To overcome this, during the nineteenth century the 'solera system' of fractional blending gradually evolved. This works on the principle that a younger wine will always take on the characteristics of a slightly older wine. One large butt or solera containing the mature sherry is the only butt from which the wine is drawn off for bottling or shipping in casks. The solera is then 'refreshed' from a *criadera* or nursery. You cannot refresh old wine with young wine, so the butt adjacent to the solera will only be a little younger than the solera wine itself. This, in turn, will be refreshed with a slightly younger wine, and so on down the line until the last butt may be refreshed with an *anada* wine that is only nine months old. Throughout its time in the *criadera* the flor continues to grow on the fino and manzanilla sherries, although during the winter months it generally dies down and sinks to the bottom of the butt to form part of the lees.

The number of butts in a *criadera* varies from as few as five to as many as fifty depending on the age and type of wine. All sherry has to be a minimum of three years old before it can be sold, but many are considerably older than this. The manzanillas and finos are generally the younger wines, while the amontillados and olorosos are older.

All sherries are basically dry wines whose sweetness is dependent on the way it is matured and the quantity of sweet wine, made from the Pedro Ximenez and Moscatel grapes, that is added to it.

Sometimes the sweet wines are blended into the sherry only months before the wine is bottled whilst in other cases they are added at the early stages of the *criadera* and mature with the sherry.

The oak casks in which the sherry is matured play an important role in the development of the characteristics of the sherry. Other woods have been tried but none imparts the same flavour to the wine. New casks are used for fermenting the sherries as this helps to season the wood and also ensures that the casks are quite clean for this important process, but butts for maturing the sherry need to be older. For some of the high-grade fino sherries, producers will not use a butt which is less than ten years old.

A meal without a glass of sherry beforehand is like a day which begins without hot sun.

Manuel M. Gonzalez Gordon

CLASSIFICATION AND QUALITY

By the time the wine is six months old, it is possible to make the first stage of classification. This is a highly skilled job, carried out by the *capataz* (foreman) of the bodega, for which a good nose and keen taste buds are essential. Wines are described as thin, fat, delicate, coarse, full, empty, etc. and the way in which the wine is developing is noted down.

To ensure that quality remains high, all sherry production is controlled by the Consejo Regulador. Founded in 1935, it is responsible for every aspect of sherry production from how the vines are planted and pruned through to the way in which the soleras are run and how the wine is bottled and exported. Severe penalties are meted out to anyone who does not conform to the highest standards, but it is only rarely that these are resorted to.

STYLES OF SHERRY

MANZANILLA

A very pale, delicate wine with a characteristic crisp aroma, manzanillas can only be produced in Sanlúcar de Barrameda. If a butt is transported to Jerez to mature, the sherry will develop into a fino. It is sometimes said that you can taste the fresh salty tang of the sea in a manzanilla, but certainly its light, dry taste is very distinctive. The alcohol content is between 15.5 and 17°.

FINO

The most popular dry sherry, fino is a pale straw colour with a crisp and delicate (almond-like) bouquet. A light wine with just a little acidity, it contains between 15.5 and 17° alcohol.

Amontillado

Sometimes referred to as 'old fino' as amontillados are naturally achieved by allowing finos to age for about eight years. The process can, however, be speeded up by increasing the alcohol content of the wine to 16.5°. An attractive amber colour, amontillado sherry is generally classified as being 'medium-dry' with a crisp (hazelnut-like) bouquet, smooth and with a full-bodied taste. The alcohol content is between 16 and 18°, but it is generally kept at below 18°for the UK market in order to avoid the higher rate of duty which wines of over 18° attract.

Oloroso

A dark golden sherry with an aromatic flavour, said to be reminiscent of walnuts. Smooth and full-bodied, in its natural state oloroso is a dry wine which is produced in exactly the same way as a fino but develops little or no flor. It is frequently sweetened with Pedro Ximenez or Moscatel wine so that the sweetness varies considerably. The alcohol content is higher than the amontillados, being between 18 and 20°.

PALO CORTADO

A type of sherry which is half-way between an amontillado and an oloroso. It has the bouquet of an amontillado, but the full flavour, colour and alcohol content of an oloroso.

CREAM SHERRY

A rich, dark golden sweet sherry made by blending oloroso with the sweet wines and allowing them to age together. As the Pedro Ximenez and Moscatel wines have a lower alcohol content, the alcohol content of these wines is generally between 18 and 20°.

FACTS AND FIGURES

The sherry region comprises 7,000 vineyards spread over an area of 17,700 hectares and the maximum density of vines per hectare is 4,100.

In 1987, total sherry production was 1,594,000 hectolitres and the total amount exported 1,006,118 hectolitres. The leading export markets are the UK – 376,518 hectolitres; Holland – 282,226 hectolitres (whose per capita consumption is the highest in the world); Germany – 165,862 hectolitres; the USA – 49,959 hectolitres; and Belgium – 41,352 hectolitres. Home consumption accounts for approximately 15% of total sales.

There are nearly 300 bodegas in the designated area and, at any one time, there are approximately 4,500,000 hectolitres of sherry maturing in crianzas. Production each year is limited to a maximum of 40% of existing stocks.

SOME CELEBRATED SHERRY HOUSES AND SHIPPERS

While an increasing quantity of sherry is shipped under the name of the off-licence chain or supermarket where it is sold, some of the old-established shippers such as Harvey, Sandeman, Gonzales Byass, Croft and Domecq remain household names. Many of the houses have very strong British connections as they were usually founded in conjunction with a British company and, over the centuries, the sherry families have intermarried so that in some tenuous way they are all related to each other.

The oldest sherry house of all is J. M. Rivero which was founded in 1650. In 1906 King Alfonso XIII of Spain asked the then head of the company, Jaquin M.ª Rivero, to visit the court of Edward VII in an effort to increase sherry sales to England which had been on the decline for several years. The visit was a great success and a substantial order was placed, but the Rivero family never cashed the cheque from Buckingham Palace and still have it in their possession!

The House of Sandeman, which is marginally better known for its port than its sherry, was founded in 1879 by a Scot, George G. Sandeman, and has been run by seven generations of the same family although it is now owned by the Seagram Company. Its trade mark of a man in a long black cloak and black matador's hat is renowned throughout the world.

The port of Bristol was an important base for many of the early shippers and by 1634 the city had given its name to a dark, sweet sherry universally known as Bristol Milk and from which Harvey's famed Bristol Cream is derived. Founded in Bristol in 1796, it was not until 1970 that Harveys bought its own bodegas in Spain, despite the company being perhaps the best known of all the sherry shippers worldwide.

Tio Pepe, produced by Gonzalez Byass, is the most celebrated dry sherry in the world, while a popular medium sherry is Dry Sack, produced by Williams and Humbert, another old British-established sherry house.

Croft are comparative newcomers to sherry, but the company originated in Oporto in 1678 from where they produced and shipped port. In 1970 they took over the bodegas and vineyards which had formerly belonged to the Gilbey family.

They often say that 'sherry is Domecq' and certainly Pedro Domecq, whose family were Huguenots from France, did more than anyone else to put the sherry industry back on its feet after the ravages brought about by the Peninsular War. Originally the firm was called Ruskin, Telford and Domecq, with Ruskin and Telford running the British end of the operation and Pedro Domecq being in charge in Jerez. Among the best-known sherries which the house produces are La Ina, Double Century and Celebration Cream. It also produces some of Spain's best brandy.

FOLKLORE AND RITUAL

In Jerez there is a saying *'las ninas y las vinas dificiles son de guarder'* – girls and vineyards are difficult to guard! The loss of a crop of carefully nurtured grapes at harvest time would be serious for the large vineyard owner, but an even greater calamity for the small peasant farmer. While more sophisticated methods are used these days, small wooden shelters called *bienteveos* ('I see you well') used to be erected on poles. Thatched with esparto grass to protect the guards from the sun, a twenty-four hour watch could then be kept in the period leading up to the harvest. In some instances on the larger estates, the guards were armed with orders to shoot to kill anyone seen stealing.

Traditionally, the vines were always manured with horse dung and it was said that a really good sherry taster could tell from the wine if a vineyard owner had cheated and used cow dung!

When a Jerezano opens a bottle of sherry, before filling the glasses he first throws a little on the ground as a token sacrifice to the earth which was the ultimate giver of the wine.

During the Great Plague (1665), one doctor who escaped totally unscathed was a Dr. Hedges who attributed his good fortune to drinking each day several glasses of sherris-sack, which he felt protected him from disease and kept up his spirits.

Well-matured casks are essential for the production of Scotch whisky and, over the centuries, a trade has developed between the whisky distillers and the sherry merchants. The whisky distillers provide the casks free to the sherry shippers who mature the sherry in them. They then ship the sherry in the casks to the UK, enabling the whisky distillers to reclaim the casks for their own use.

When tasting sherry in the bodegas, the *capataz* uses a special cup on a long handle called a *venencia* which he is able to dip into the butt without destroying the flor. With one deft movement, he then pours the sherry into a number of glasses for tasting – an apparently effortless manoeuvre but one that takes considerable practice.

LA FIESTA
DE LA VENDIMIA

The start of the grape harvest has always been heralded by small fiestas, mounted in true Spanish style with flamenco dancers and bull fights, but since 1948 the fiesta in Jerez has been a much larger and grander affair.

Held over the weekend nearest to 8 September, every year it is dedicated to a different sherry-drinking nation. The mayor of the capital city of that country usually attends as the guest of honour and for several days a carnival atmosphere prevails throughout the entire region.

The programme varies slightly from year to year, but on the first day the Queen of the Vintage, together with her attendants, drives in procession through the streets of Jerez to the Plaza de Arenal. The floats are decked with flowers, some of which are thrown to the people lining the streets, together with sweets for the children. This is followed by a display of fireworks in the evening and a banquet, which does not start until ten o'clock and goes on until the early hours of the morning.

Parties are given by the various merchants and sherry shippers at their bodegas or warehouses, not only in Jerez but in Sanlúcar de Barrameda and El Puerto de Santa Maria over the next couple of days, and the whole event culminates in a ceremony at the Collegiate Church in Jerez.

One of the old wooden *lagars* or presses is set up in front of the church and, after the grapes have been blessed by the priest, four workmen wearing the traditional studded boots begin to tread the grapes. Just as the first drops of juice or must appear, an army of white doves is released to fly all over Spain to announce the good news that the sherry harvest has begun.

STORING SHERRIES

Once bottled, the fino and manzanilla sherries should be drunk as soon as possible so they should always be bought from a wine merchant or off-licence with a high turnover. Nor do they keep well once opened – three days is generally considered to be the optimum time although they can be kept for up to ten if well-stoppered in a refrigerator. Unlike normal dry white wines they do not become vinegary after opening, but they quickly oxidise and lose their fragrance and freshness.

The sweeter sherries will slowly continue maturing in the bottle with the sugar gradually turning to alcohol, so that after a period of many years a slightly drier sherry is achieved with a fuller flavour. Once opened, the creams and sweet olorosos will keep for a month while the amontillados are best kept for just a couple of weeks.

HOW TO SERVE SHERRY

Sherry should not be drunk out of the typical 'schooner' glass used in most British pubs as this completely destroys the bouquet of the wine. Tulip-shaped 'copita' glasses (the sort generally used for serving white wine) are much better. The glass should be filled only about one third to a half full, and it is then possible to appreciate fully the bouquet and flavour.

The dry sherries – the manzanillas and finos – should always be served well chilled. In Spain it is quite usual to serve sherry in a tumbler 'on the rocks' with a few ice cubes added to the glass, and the sweeter amontillados and creams as well as the dry sherries can be served in this way.

Long Sherry Drinks

At one time it was considered sacrilege to serve sherry in any way other than straight from the bottle. While this would be true for some of the very fine vintage sherries, ordinary sherries can be used to make some delicious and very refreshing long drinks.

SHERRY SPRITZER: Both dry and sweet sherries can be mixed with soda water or sparkling mineral water to make a spritzer. Pour the sherry into the glass, add a couple of ice cubes and a slice of lemon, then top up with water – the exact proportions can vary according to taste from 50:50 to 25:75 sherry and water.

SHERRY WITH LEMONADE: A popular mixture in Australia, but you need to use a sweet cream sherry for this. Pour a measure of sherry into a glass, add a couple of ice cubes and a good squeeze of orange juice, then top up with lemonade.

SHERRY WITH TONIC WATER: An unusual combination which works surprisingly well and for which dry or sweet sherry can be used. Pour a measure of sherry into a glass, add a twist of lemon rind, then top up with tonic water.

'Sherry, the civilised drink.'

Somerset Maugham

SHERRY VINEGAR

Years ago it was quite common for a few butts of sherry to turn to vinegar during fermentation because of accidental exposure to bacteria. The Andalusians valued this vinegar highly for dressing their salads. With the careful control that is now possible, it is rare for a butt to turn to vinegar and sherry vinegar is generally made specifically from the poorest quality wines. It has a slightly nutty flavour which enhances any dressing and it is also excellent used in simple reduced sauces such as the Beef Strips with Spring Onions and Almonds on page 51.

SHERRY RECIPES

CONSOMMÉ JULIENNE

The addition of some fino sherry to a can of consommé transforms it immediately from a rather mundane canned soup into something quite special. Other meat soups such as game soups also benefit from this treatment and a chilled manzanilla or fino are the classic accompaniment to them.

1 carrot
1 small turnip
1 small leek
salt
2 × 15 oz (425 g) cans consommé
1/4 pint (150 ml) fino sherry
freshly ground black pepper

Peel the carrot and turnip and clean the leek thoroughly, discarding the outside leaves. Cut into very fine matchsticks or julienne strips. Bring a small pan of salted water to the boil, add the vegetables, cook for 2 minutes, then drain thoroughly.

Tip into a clean pan, together with the consommé and sherry. Bring to just below boiling point, taste and adjust seasoning, then pour into soup bowls and serve at once with crisp toast.

Serves 4–6

SPANISH WARM SALAD

A perfect light starter for a dinner party, to which the sherry vinegar gives a pleasant, slightly nutty tang.

about 8 oz (225 g) mixed salad leaves (endive, radic-chio, lettuce hearts)
1 ripe avocado
1 red pepper
1 chorizo, weighing approximately 5 oz (150 g)
1 tablespoon olive oil

For the dressing:
6 tablespoons virgin olive oil
2 tablespoons sherry vinegar
1 teaspoon mild French or Spanish mustard
salt
freshly ground black pepper

Thoroughly wash the salad leaves. Divide between six plates, cover with clingfilm and refrigerate until ready to serve.

Put all the ingredients for the dressing into a screw-topped jar and shake well. Shortly before serving, peel the avocado, cut into slices and arrange on the salad leaves. Halve the pepper, remove the seeds and cut into thin strips.

Cut the chorizo into ¼ inch (6 mm) cubes. Heat the olive oil in a small frying pan and gently fry the red pepper for about 3 minutes, then add the chorizo and continue cooking for a further 3 minutes. Scatter the chorizo and red pepper over the avocado and salad leaves on the plates, pour over the dressing and serve at once.

Serves 6

CHINESE RAW FISH STRIPS

While not as popular in China as it is in Japan, raw fish still features in Chinese cookery. In this recipe the fish is lightly marinated in a mixture of sesame oil, sherry and soy sauce before serving.

1 lb (450 g) plaice fillets
2 spring onions, finely chopped
1 tablespoon sesame oil
2 tablespoons fino sherry
2 tablespoons soy sauce
salt
freshly ground black pepper
1 slice fresh pineapple

Skin the fish and cut into narrow strips about 2 inches (5 cm) long. Place the onions, oil, sherry, soy sauce and seasoning in a shallow dish. Add the fish, toss well and leave for 30 minutes.

Lift the fish out of the marinade and arrange on a serving dish. Shred the pineapple very finely and scatter over the top.

Serves 4

SWEETBREADS IN SHERRY SAUCE

A Spanish way of cooking sweetbreads which is very quick and easy. Serve as a starter or main course.

1 lb (450 g) sweetbreads
salt
1 teaspoon lemon juice
2 oz (50 g) butter
5 tablespoons amontillado sherry
freshly ground black pepper
1/4 pint (150 ml) double cream
2 oz (50 g) smoked ham, finely chopped

Soak the sweetbreads in cold water for 1–2 hours, changing the water a couple of times. Drain and cut away the thick membranes. Put into a pan, cover with cold water, add a teaspoon of salt and lemon juice and bring to the boil. Cook gently for 15 minutes, then drain thoroughly. Place the sweetbreads between two plates with a weight on top to press them and leave for at least 15 minutes.

Melt the butter in a pan, add the sweetbreads and cook for 5 minutes or until lightly browned. Pour over the sherry, season with salt and pepper and cook for 2–3 minutes. Remove the sweetbreads with a draining spoon, place in a serving dish and keep warm. Add the cream to the pan and bring to the boil. Taste and adjust seasoning, pour the sauce over the sweetbreads, then sprinkle with the ham.

Serves 3–6

QUEEN SCALLOPS, SPANISH-STYLE

Little frozen queen scallops have a superb flavour, and they are often as little as half the price of the larger ones. Cooked here in a delicate manzanilla sherry, they make a delicious main course served with saffron rice and salad.

2 shallots, finely chopped
2 sprigs fresh tarragon or 1 teaspoon dried tarragon
¼ pint (150 ml) manzanilla sherry
1 lb (450 g) frozen Queen scallops, thawed
¼ pint (150 ml) double cream
salt
freshly ground black pepper

Put the shallots and tarragon into a pan with the sherry and bring to the boil. Add the scallops to the pan, cover and simmer gently just until the scallops become opaque – on no account should they be overcooked.

Remove from the pan with a draining spoon, place on a heated serving dish and keep warm. Boil the liquor in the pan until it is reduced by half, then stir in the cream and heat gently. Discard the sprigs of tarragon, if used, then season to taste with salt and pepper. Pour the sauce over the scallops and serve as soon as possible.

Serves 4

Eliza Acton's Sausage Cakes With Chestnuts

Sherry was not only a popular drink in Victorian England, but was also used extensively in the cookery of the time. It is essential that a good-quality sausagemeat with a low fat content is used when making this dish, otherwise the sauce will end up too fatty.

15 fresh chestnuts
1 lb (450 g) good-quality sausagemeat
1 rounded tablespoon seasoned flour
1/2 oz (15 g) butter
1/2 pint (300 ml) beef or chicken stock
1/4 pint (150 ml) fino sherry
1 bouquet garni
salt
freshly ground black pepper

Make a slit in the chestnuts, put them into a pan of boiling water for 5 minutes, then drain. When cool enough to handle, peel off the outer shell and the brown skin.

Form the sausagemeat into four flat cakes and toss them in the seasoned flour. Melt the butter in a frying pan with a lid and gently fry the sausagemeat cakes on both sides until golden brown. Lift out with a fish slice and put on one side. Add the stock, sherry and bouquet garni to the pan and bring to the boil. Replace the sausagemeat cakes, add the chestnuts, cover the pan and simmer very gently for 1 hour.

Lift the sausagemeat cakes out of the pan with a fish slice and arrange on a serving plate. Discard the bouquet garni and skim off any excess fat from the sauce. Taste and adjust seasoning, then pour over the cakes together with the chestnuts.

Serves 4

CHINESE CHICKEN WITH PEAS AND LETTUCE

Sherry is frequently used in Chinese recipes in place of rice wine which is more difficult to obtain. It makes an excellent substitute which many people even prefer.

2 large chicken breast fillets
salt
freshly ground black pepper
1 egg white
2 tablespoons cornflour
4 tablespoons oil
1 lettuce heart, shredded
2 cloves garlic, crushed
3 spring onions, chopped
4 oz (100 g) fresh or frozen peas
2 tablespoons fino sherry

Cut the chicken into strips about ¼ inch (6 mm) wide. Season them with salt and pepper. Taking two or three strips at a time, dip them first in the egg white and then toss in the cornflour. Place on a plate until all the strips have been coated.

Heat 2 tablespoons of the oil in a wok or large frying pan and fry the chicken slices over a moderate heat until they turn opaque. Remove from the pan with a slotted spoon and put on one side. Increase the heat, add a further tablespoon of oil to the pan, and when this is hot add the lettuce. Sprinkle with about ¼ teaspoon of salt and cook for about 30 seconds, stirring all the time until the lettuce has wilted. Remove from the pan with a slotted spoon and place in a warm serving dish.

Add the remaining tablespoon of oil to the pan, then the garlic and onions, and cook for a minute. Return the chicken slices to the pan with the peas and cook, stirring, for a further minute. Pour in the sherry and season to taste. Spoon over the lettuce in the serving dish and serve as soon as possible.

Serves 3–4

CHICKEN JOINTS WITH TOMATOES AND MUSHROOMS

Sherry adds an interesting and subtle flavour to casseroles such as this. As sherry does not keep well once opened, it is an excellent way of using up a small quantity left in the bottle or decanter.

4 chicken joints
salt
freshly ground black pepper
2 tablespoons olive oil
1 large onion, peeled and finely chopped
2 cloves garlic, crushed
14 oz (400 g) can tomatoes, roughly chopped
8 oz (225 g) cup mushrooms, roughly chopped
1 tablespoon chopped fresh oregano or 1 teaspoon dried
    oregano
1/4 pint (150 ml) dry oloroso or amontillado sherry

Season the chicken joints with salt and pepper. Heat the oil in a large pan, add the chicken joints and fry until crisp and golden brown. Remove from the heat and put on one side.

Add the onion and garlic to the pan and cook gently for 5 minutes, then add the tomatoes, mushrooms, oregano and sherry and bring to the boil. Replace the chicken joints, cover the pan and simmer gently for 1 hour. Skim off any excess fat, and taste and adjust seasoning before serving.

Serves 4

BEEF STRIPS WITH SPRING ONIONS AND ALMONDS

The addition of a little sherry vinegar gives flavour to this sauce and reduces any greasiness.

1½ lb (675 g) good-quality rump steak
salt
freshly ground black pepper
2 oz (50 g) butter
2 tablespoons vegetable oil
1 inch (2.5 cm) piece fresh ginger root, peeled and very
*   finely chopped*
6 spring onions, finely chopped
2 oz (50 g) blanched almonds, finely chopped
2 tablespoons sherry vinegar

Cut the meat into strips about ¼ inch (6 mm) thick and 2 inches (5 cm) long. Season them with salt and pepper. Heat the butter and oil in a large frying pan and quickly fry the steak until well browned. Remove from the pan with a slotted spoon, put on one side and keep warm.

Lower the heat in the pan and gently fry the ginger, spring onions and almonds for about 3 minutes. Pour over the sherry vinegar and cook for a further minute, stirring all the time. Taste and adjust the seasoning, then spoon over the meat and serve at once.

Serves 4

HAM AND SHERRY MOUSSE

A good buffet party dish, this recipe from Wiltshire dates from the early nineteenth century and can be served as either a starter or a main course.

1 oz (25 g) butter
1 oz (25 g) flour
½ pint (300 ml) milk
3 eggs, separated
¼ pint (150 ml) fino sherry
1 rounded tablespoon chopped parsley
4 spring onions, finely chopped
1 lb (450 g) cooked bacon or ham, minced
¼ pint (150 ml) single cream
½ oz (15 g) powdered gelatine
4 tablespoons water
salt
freshly ground black pepper
¼ teaspoon grated nutmeg

To garnish:
slices of cucumber

Melt the butter in a pan, stir in the flour and cook for a minute, then gradually stir in the milk. Bring to the boil, stirring all the time, then remove from the heat and stir in the egg yolks. Gradually beat in the sherry, then stir in the parsley, spring onions and bacon or ham. Mix well and stir in the cream.

Sprinkle the gelatine over the water in a basin and leave to soften for 5 minutes, then stand the basin over a pan of hot water and leave until the gelatine has dissolved. Beat into the ham mixture. Add the nutmeg and season to taste with salt and pepper. Whisk the egg whites until they form soft peaks and fold into the mixture. Turn into a serving dish and leave for at least 4 hours or until the mixture is thoroughly set. Garnish with slices of cucumber before serving.

Serves 10–15

KENTISH OAST CAKES

Up until the Second World War, hop-picking for-med the annual paid holiday for many Cockneys, whose love of a good tipple of sherry is widely renowned! Whole families, including babes in arms and grandparents, would travel out to the hop fields of Kent in late August and early September, where they would set up camps, either in tents or in empty barns. Much of the cooking was done over an open fire, and these little warm cakes were popular teatime fare at the end of a busy day out in the fresh country air.

Quick and simple to prepare, Oast Cakes are the perfect thing to cook up if people drop in unexpec-tedly at teatime. Served with fresh cream, they can even make a simple dessert.

8 oz (225 g) plain flour
½ teaspoon salt
1 teaspoon baking powder
½ teaspoon mixed spice
2 oz (50 g) lard
3 oz (75 g) currants
1 tablespoon caster sugar
4 tablespoons sherry
2 tablespoons water
vegetable oil for frying
caster sugar for dredging

Sift the flour, salt, baking powder and spice into a bowl. Rub in the lard until the mixture is crumbly, then add the currants and sugar. Bind together with the sherry and water into a stiff dough. Form the dough into balls about the size of a golf ball, then flatten these out to make small, round cakes just over ½ inch (about 1.5 cm) thick.

Shallow-fry the cakes in hot oil for about 8 minutes, turning once. Take care that the fat is not too hot or the outside of the cakes will become over-browned before the dough is fully cooked through. Remove the cakes from the pan, drain thoroughly on kitchen paper, then dredge with caster sugar and serve warm.

Makes about 12

SHERRY TRIFLE

There is a world of difference between a sherry trifle made with sponge cakes, sandwiched together with good-quality jam, soaked with a cream or oloroso sherry, covered with a home-made egg custard and finally topped with fresh whipped cream, and the poor imitations which are all too often served up.

8 trifle sponge cakes
6 rounded tablespoons high-quality strawberry or raspberry jam
1/4 pint (150 ml) cream or sweet oloroso sherry
1/2 pint (300 ml) milk
3 eggs, lightly beaten
1 oz (25 g) vanilla sugar
1/2 pint (300 ml) double cream

To decorate:
1 oz (25 g) blanched almonds
a few cherries
strips of angelica

Split the trifle sponges in half and spread with the jam. Place in a glass or other suitable serving dish. Pour over the sherry and leave the sponges to soak for at least 1 hour.

Bring the milk to blood heat in a saucepan. Combine the eggs with the sugar in a basin and beat lightly together. Pour over the milk and beat well, then strain into the top of a double boiler or basin placed over a pan of hot water. Cook gently until the mixture coats the back of a wooden spoon. Remove from the heat and leave to cool for about 10 minutes, stirring frequently, then pour over the sponge cakes. Leave for at least 4 hours or until the custard is quite cold.

Whip the cream until it holds its shape, then spread all over the top of the custard. Lightly toast the almonds under a moderate grill, then chop roughly. Scatter the almonds over the top of the trifle, and decorate with a few cherries and pieces of angelica.

Serves 6–8

OLD ENGLISH SYLLABUB

The word 'syllabub' is a corruption of Sill, a region of the Champagne country which produced sparkling wine known as Sill or Sille, and 'bub' which was the common Elizabethan slang expression for a bubbling drink. Sill was mixed with frothing cream or bub – hence syllabub. By the middle of the eighteenth century, it was more usual to make it with sherry, a little brandy and cream. It was from the syllabub that trifle was developed.

1 lemon
6 tablespoons cream or sweet oloroso sherry plus 2 table-
  spoons brandy (or use all sherry)
3 oz (75 g) caster sugar
½ pint (300 ml) double cream

Thinly pare the rind from the lemon, put it into a basin and pour over the sherry and brandy if using. Squeeze the juice from the lemon, add to the bowl then cover and leave for at least 6 hours, or preferably overnight.

Strain the liquid into a clean bowl, add the sugar and stir until dissolved. Add the cream, then whisk until the mixture stands in soft peaks. Pile into glasses and chill until ready to serve.

Serves 6

ACKNOWLEDGEMENTS

The author and publisher would like to acknowledge the help of the following:

The Sherry Institute of Spain
Linford Wines, Newmarket

OTHER TITLES IN THE SERIES

The Little Green Avocado Book
The Little Garlic Book
The Little Pepper Book
The Little Lemon Book
The Little Mustard Book
The Little Honey Book
The Little Nut Book
The Little Mushroom Book
The Little Rice Book
The Little Tea Book
The Little Coffee Book
The Little Chocolate Book
The Little Curry Book
The Little Mediterranean Food Book
The Little Exotic Vegetable Book
The Little Exotic Fruit Book
The Little Yoghurt Book
The Little Tofu Book
The Little Breakfast Book
The Little Egg Book
The Little Potato Book
The Little Spice Book
The Little Herb Book